SNOW NEGATIVES

First published in 2007 by
The Dedalus Press
13 Moyclare Road
Baldoyle
Dublin 13
Ireland

www.dedaluspress.com

ISBN 978 1 904556 85 5

Dedalus Press titles are represented in North America
by Syracuse University Press, Inc., 621 Skytop Road,
Suite 110, Syracuse, New York 13244, and in the UK by
Central Books, 99 Wallis Road, London E9 5LN

Printed and bound in the UK by Lightning Source,
6 Precedent Drive, Rooksley, Milton Keynes MK13 8PR, UK.

Typeset by Beth Romano

Cover image © Kuzma

The Dedalus Press receives financial assistance from
An Chomhairle Ealaíon / The Arts Council, Ireland

SNOW NEGATIVES

Enda Coyle-Greene

22/u/7

To Anne
with love & best
wishes for your own
work!

Enda

Dedalus

THANKS

The author would especially like to thank the following: Pat Boran, Jonathan Williams, Bernadette Coyle-Stewart, Thornfield Poets, Skerries Women's Writing Group, Linda McLoughlin, Aileen Morrissey, Aileen Kelly, The Tyrone Guthrie Centre at Annaghmakerrig and The Patrick Kavanagh Society.

ACKNOWLEDGEMENTS

Acknowlededgements are due to the editors of the following where some of these poems were previously published or broadcast: *AIDS West*, *Asylum*, *Books Ireland*, *The Burning Bush*, *Bray Arts Journal*, *The Cork Literary Review*, *Crannog*, *Cyphers*, *Envoi*, *The Echoing Years*, *Fortnight*, *Incognito*, *Podium II*, *Poetry Ireland Review*, *Riposte*, *The SHoP*, *The Stinging Fly* and *The Sunday Tribune*; and the producers of the RTÉ Radio 1 programmes *Rattlebag*, *Sunday Miscellany* and *The Enchanted Way*.

For My Family

Contents

⁓

SNOW NEGATIVES

Road Sign

From a distance
I think it's a cat,
a black cat, a sign
and a good one at that.

But then as I get near
it sees me, turns
back in
towards whatever

wildness seeded it
beside the motorway:
a baby fox,
on tenuous, inked legs,

skittering away.

Rage

for Ivy Bannister

All day, I've measured space
and distance, how we land-bridge countries, move
through air, cross water, quantify
the gaps between one city
and the next.

And now I'm in my car. The radio won't play
the usual music. Voices rise and fall,
crawl out from underneath two buildings
I can hear collapse
on air.

I don't want to meet anyone. I want to be home
and so I skirt Balheary.
It's Indian summer, a glorious cliché;
only hay bales, rolled and ready,
tight and tidy

in the fields as rows of soldiers, guard the start of autumn;
insinuating bladed winds, winter's ice, a skid
beneath my wheels. On the road
there's nothing else behind me
or before me:

am I the only one alive? Suddenly a car breathes
on my back: square, sleek, silver. Smoke-black
windows hide the driver's face, but I can see
the hairs stand on his arm, the clamp
of his hand.

I want to stop, get out, say, Don't you know your way
around here? You couldn't know these lanes the way I do:
they're narrow, twisted, liable
to spring a blind surprise
on you.

Take your time. You. I'm not going to evaporate
to let you pass, or fly into the ditch, thick with nettles, rats.
I only want what you want. You'll have to wait.
Will the world fold, crashing, burning,
screaming to its end

if you and I are late tonight?

September 11, 2001

Laura Nyro's Window

Morning surprises her:
sucked from the sky
over Gibsom Street,
fragile and hollow,
it waits at her window.

She watches the city sleep
fall off the skyscrapers, canyons
in clouds that have burst
in the night
unnoticed.

A pool on the balcony
mirrors the broken sky:
it glistens, one tear
in the huge blue
eye of a giant.

Witches

It was dark then.
We walked like witches through town,
out of the suburbs
into the unknown,
unknowing.

We were pure—
in our hearts, in our words,
in our deeds:
while the slow ash of innocence clung
to the cigarettes we smoked
behind the bicycle sheds.

We would all burn later.

As it was, we were fools,
unkissed by the light
bright smile of the sun,
only happy when sad,
aching for boys
who were mad, bad,
dangerous to know.

Some of whom were poets.

Some lived in the woods, singing
songs in the bandstand, hymns for the high altar
sung to a tree, a one-legged hill cloud.

Some were working-class heroes.

And we circled the lake
as our skirts dragged the ground
to draw a dull glitter
up through the dirty snow:
circles and circles completed, crow-black,
while the bell called the darkness down
over St. Stephen's Green.

The moon washed the roofs
as we flew around the city, or danced
around our shoulder bags
(Saturday nights at the *Os*).
We were senseless as stones, as the birds
in the sky,
only living to fly.

We would all come down.
Later.

So Many

We never noticed you,
although our placid moon-round faces
felt the furnace heat of yours
too close.

You invented lives for us: lies
of mythical additions and omissions,
where we became so many
heroines. We never knew
the meaning of the word; still,
you persisted in naming us
thus.

      But ask yourselves
where we are now. We didn't rot
beneath an unforgiving earth, no death
or birth attended us, or offered us
the chance to leg it
out of there, out of the blue front door,
away from you.

Click.

Hard lids shuttered our dull eyes,
and so we never saw
your worn all-summer cotton clothes,
your whitened-over, scuffed Communion shoes,
or you, arrayed like us in rows:
like us, so many dolls.

All morning, rain

All morning, rain has stained the cobblestones
the colour of the sky,
the colour of the spirit
store's grey-slated roof, framed
in one sash window, then another;
you reel between them, high
above the yard, glassed into eight square rooms
over a public house.

She is waiting for the rain to pass:
you can hear her shutting cupboards, cutting off
the knives' dull clamour,
you can hear her
putting out the air.

She's not looking at the hill, as you are
now; she doesn't see the light that breaks
the clouds above the sullen trees
or the houses there
that will, one day, be visible
from all across the village,
from the surface
of the moon.

The back kitchen door scolds the floor
as she goes out, as the wind in that instant
skims the stairs,
to fold around the silence
of her absence.

Your hawed breath
hardens on the glass that separates
that year from this.
She lifts the latch
and shifts the wicket gate:
the garden, winter-dead,
receives her.

Vertigo

In memory of my father

It's not the only thing you left me,
this free-falling, light-headed lurch
towards nothing in particular.
Nor is it the best
you could have wished for me:
that I should be gripped
by the same plain fear
you couldn't even name
in the end.

In the end
I tried to sound it out for you,
looking down from my great height,
feeling two seasons shake
this tree,
this monstrous, bluey-green
undying obscenity,
my toes curled at the thought of flight.

No, it was never your intention
to leave me, to go like that, stepping off into air
the colour of your honest eyes,
quietly surprised at first, I imagine,
by the ease with which you went
spinning down
as the ground came up,
while the wind sang the years
backwards
in your head.

Snow Negatives

RAHILLY CASTLE: MORNING

My eyes snap open on his old man's stare, a snare
to keep me watching him
beyond the glass.
His running colours heal
the frost-hard winter grass, the barren stones
my sister, sleeping, dreams about.
Nothing else moves.
The water at the pump still
thickens into ice, becomes a mirror
for the pregnant sky.
I cry to my own child
Come and see the hare.
In air,
another child answers.

GORT: MIDDAY

A door creaks as an old man
folds the cold outside him
with his overcoat and wonders
if the day will hold. He asks me
how I am. He has
the same eyes as my father,
the same unclouded
country face:
he has lived
forever in this place.

GALWAY: DUSK

The cathedral swells to fill
the rear-view mirror,
a pillar of salt.
On the left a petrol station
is a brazen light; on the right,
trees dip their silver heads
and shiver.

THE ORANMORE ROAD: NIGHT

Later, when I read in the papers about the old man
murdered in his house
on the Oranmore Road, I remember
a house, square as a child's drawing,
with a fence that stretched out
on either side
and a chimney from which smoke also stretched and then froze:
an apron of snow
for a garden,
and no footprints
coming in
or going out.

Radio Geography

He had lived there once,
on his way through the midlands
to the city. I could hear *Athlone*
in his voice, in the way he told me to
Lower that radio

as I spun the dial across
the broad yellow face;
the black stick-pupil of the station-
marker made a tiger's eye
at every place I stopped

to catch the music. Athlone
was easy, easier than Hilversum.
I asked my dad where that was;
when he told me, I imagined
clogs and flaxen plaits, a boy

who'd kept an ocean out,
his finger wrinkled, waterlogged.
Kneeling on the armchair, leaning
into hissing gaps between the names
of places I could go to,

I knew what was there: seas
that waited to be reeled in, waves,
still miles away, but here
with me, the unmapped radio
geography of air.

Postcards

I'd say this station café hasn't changed
since the 'forties, on the walls the same framed views
       fade in an order
I'd say this station café hasn't changed.

The train to Zürich doesn't stop:
blotting light, it leeches air between the platforms
       in a drawn-out scream.
The train to Zürich doesn't stop,

the window shivers, licked by ice
that sticks like sugar-spit, then swells to opaque crystal
       bleached by snow again;
the window shivers, licked by ice.

Late afternoon intrudes, slides in
behind another tourist as the door is shouldered open
       on an almost empty room;
late afternoon intrudes, slides in.

I bite my pen. I swallow words
like coffee cloud-swirls stirred to warm depths, sweet
       but bitter in the after-taste:
I bite my pen. I swallow words:

It's beautiful but cold. Today
my eyelids fused as I stood and shook my boots off
       underneath the cable car.
It's beautiful but cold. Today

a tear froze on my face
as I listened to a band play tunes I didn't know but knew
        you would have known;
a tear froze on my face.

Outside, the paths have frosted cauls
that break beneath returning boots as the last lift empties
        and the silence ends
outside; the paths have frosted cauls.

The earth is harder six feet under
snow that silts in pleated shadows on the mountain, *colder*
        where you sleep.
The earth is harder six feet under.

Earlier that day

*After seeing a photograph of F. Scott Fitzgerald,
taken towards the end of his life*

Earlier that day, cut by the light
in the bathroom at nine a.m.,
he had bled, thin blood
mapping out the razor's edge, naming
a course across his mirrored face.

Shaking, he had stooped to trap
resisting water in the sink. Thrown
into his eyes, it forced the lashes there
to separate, divide like lovers' hands
or early stars surprised.

The folded towel gave up
its swollen comfort as he'd opened it
and laid it out, still warm,
across the fingers he had splayed
and readied to obliterate, to numb;

so that later, in the studio,
there was nothing left of him, no trace
of his stare to be sieved through hard glass
by the aspic glare of the camera's
hooded, sudden eye.

Ornithology in Doheny and Nesbitt's

It was dark in the bar that night, but we were talking about the day-lit
owl that flashed through branches overhead as I drove to the gate—
        not a flicker

in its reach, more of an expanse than I would have thought possible,
I said—and you agreed that neither one of us had ever seen an owl
        except as drawn from life, as wooden

as the key-ring fob brought back to me from Greece, its belly etched
in red ink with my initials and my mobile number, my personal
        talisman.

I couldn't understand why seeing it had made me happy, as if the rush
of beating wings had somehow owned the power to break my heart,
        or make it whole,

and I told you how I'd listened to the same sound grounded, stinging
in its frantic uselessness within walls; in the guileless air outside,
        another country, a blessed galaxy

it escaped to through the sudden ardent softness of an open window.
Later, as I'd waited for the light to leave the sky—not lonely, I said,
        not really, just quiet—

in the space between what is safe and what might only be described
as sinister, other voices, other birds, tricked kindness off the witch-
        dense, painted woods;

above the rest, the echo-stressed vocabulary of the cuckoo calling time
across a distance left me with no sense of what its message meant,
        if it had one,

if it was an omen like the owl was once for Rome, or a *piseog* —
a malevolence swept into panicked wings that have been trapped
      indoors—

you wondered too: you said you didn't know, but I kept asking, asking,
thinking of a hawk I've never spoken of, that tested gravity on air
      while all below was melded

to an under-map of moss on stone, the warp and weft of meadow grass.
I watched it for what seemed to me the longest breath I've ever held
      before the spell broke

open and the world became an island, its beaches chalked outlines
around a body: I'm still not certain why it dived, or how or when
      it was

that I had realised its eyes—like flinting glass in sunlight sharpened
all that swift way down—could see the shape of everything, the state
      of me.

Self-Portrait

for Mary Donnelly

You do not become
what the air insists
you have always been
for the time you are here
to breathe it. As it is

you are everything
the mirror has gleaned
from the evidence given
on a basis of one day, some day,
now. The light twists

as you look at what is there—
a turn of your head
throws a profile past
the slanted inner corner
of your blue eye. That liar.

Hope

She has a sense of somewhere beyond
here where there is hope. A note cools
on a piano in a room long emptied,
and so well that only the ghosts notice.
She is aware of them all; they catch her
breathing now and then, attempting to
turn around again in a space that grows
narrow but not bitter with age:
the night's end-stage perhaps, its black edge
stopped dead by a sliver of morning
light; the certainty of sorts of a day
where something, anything, might happen.
Oscillating, she assumes the shape, skin-
slipping to a place where she can wait.

Grafton Street

For a while, the closed hours ticked
in the dark between the clothes rails,
waited as the air stilled to tissue
paper folds, carefully
creased into place.

The shutter flickered as dreams turned
uneasily behind it: an eyelid
between what is real
and what can be bought
and carried off

or worn by the mannequins that hold
their aching poses by the escalator;
each raised arm a cold stone
wing on a graveyard angel
dressed for flight.

But now, the day is opening again.
The light is a colour that runs and keeps
running—it has to be returned; it seeps
in as the metal stretches
and the door is unlocked

and the sound of the street slips past
the security man, to whom it seems as if
the city never slept; he barely notices
that the gutters are coated
in dust the wind will lift

to send the way of blown skirts,
all over the slow, curved hill of the street.
The sea can be felt then, its salt pressed
to air-shades, invisible
among the roof slates.

The shop assistant arriving for work
walks in as white fluorescence stutters, fits:
unpacked, unfolded, taken out,
her day ahead is a shirt,
still pinned.

Opium

for Vanessa

This is how it will be.

A large dog, yellow, I think,
will shake himself free
of a river, a sea.

Before he is dry
he will run to you, cloaked
in a river, a different sea.

Sometime, in winter perhaps,
you'll shift a screen of curtain,
sift the night

through an open window,
lean across your kitchen sink
to lift a cat in, black,

I imagine. His fur will be
short, dense,
filled with fog.

You'll breathe him in, and in
your present tense
think only of your past.

Some day, somewhere
in a city I can't see,
a woman will pass

you in a crowd; drugged
by her perfume, the heady scent
she will leave after her,

you won't struggle as you fall
back to now:
and you will remember me

telling you this.

Pineforest

I look up her number in the book,
there aren't too many there,
five or six at most:
none of them admit
to her identifying initial.
Will I call? I could listen to her voice
in safety, untraceable
at someone else's desk. Silent
as a shut drawer
in a deserted office,

dust circles in a shaft of sunlight,
mocks the day's progression
over folders and the brown box files
with my handwriting on them,
making me wince.
There is an obscenity involved
in such honesty, an exposure of souls
in the looped Ls, in the Os
closed tighter than his arm
around her shoulder in the photograph.

I turn it over in my hand. In my head
the dead syllables prickle;
two names, the place-words slurred
to one where two should be:
Pineforest.

It is black and white.
It is all so obvious.

I look again. My finger nails
the names' disinterested declarations
of innocence.

It has nothing to do with us, they say,
betraying nothing I could use as evidence.
I close the book. I put away
the photograph's most telling lie:
if she had cared
to look beyond the trees, beyond
the slanted summer sky,
she would have seen me there:
a glimmer in his eye.

Another Moon

It could have been the beauty of the moon
that drew him in
towards the open window. Other insects pulled
against the seeping night, were pinned
against the glass: thinner-skinned,
the kitchen light dissected them.

Perhaps the never-bolted back door squealed
on unoiled hinges and alerted him.
My father, sleeping off
the television's squeezed white dot,
had the sound turned down. I never heard
the moon blow out
another moon

into a puddle in the field behind our house;
mud stopping where its round white O
sluiced stagnant water. I only saw
the mirror of the moon
move out from where it lay and leave
a loosened image floating
bald and white

as a man's bare head with a hand that clawed
against the high back wall. I could only listen
to the hiss, the thump
thump thumping of her
cool reluctant iron: a dull
and far away gun

going off, somewhere.

Finis Terrae

It takes me quickly, by surprise
in the middle of the street
that could be anywhere.

I step out of noise
and rain, my heart forgets a beat
it has kept since air,

displacing water, pulsed my rise
through new light out of older heat,
held me there.

A voice behind my eyes
tells it will end, and where, repeats
and keeps repeating, *Finisterre.*

The Long Woman's Grave

It is as easy as drawing breath
with you: in and out
and in thin words
you paint a big picture,
a promise of silence.

You draw yourself along my height:
my long bones dissolve
with your bones, stones
and the dry hard heat
of days behind me now.

Stars stiffen into position
over our heads: space
stretches out to die
beyond this bed,
that open door,

the valley.

*The Long Woman's Grave in Omeath, County Louth is
reputedly the last resting place of a Spanish woman who
died of a broken heart after being lured to the mountain-
ringed valley by her Irish lover, who had promised her land,
"as far as your eye can see."*

In Latin, to the lake

i. glacialis

It was never hers to appropriate
and she has no idea of its depths
where light takes down the leavings of the sky
through layers of air in late afternoon
in January. The emptiness stalls,
just long enough for her to be aware
of what had happened in the month before
she looks, and sees that nothing is the same;
she's lifting mist with the back of her glove
from the window of a car that pulls her
on towards a place she's never been,
to what was there beside the crooked road:
a field in almost-dark, the lake, its face
ice-cauled and scraped—like happiness, heart-shaped.

ii. oculus plenus

Cornered between windows, the view she takes
from one is easily complete, a hedge
around a carefully grown shrubbery,
a gravel path, a roof under repair.
The eyeful of lake is different though;
there is nothing that is not tenuous
about the man, the boat, the impetus
that is created, as rain, jittery
at encountering water, becomes more.
Landed, she is looking as he steps off
on the other shore, an evanescence
quickening in a tangle of dark trees;
when she has almost turned away again
he picks up something she will never see.

iii. camera obscura

In the time, the only time that it can take
for her to turn around, the sun stumbles.
Blind in its fall, she waits beyond the gaze
its glazed ambivalence stops level
with her breath, her heartbeat, on the same high
space that chimneys, roof slates, winter birds hold.
She folds into herself inside her coat
in a silence that allows her listen
to the eye-lock. Light within its frame
is music, other voices on a street
she knows is near, which won't be, can't be, kept
as anything but image; nothing's clear
except the lake, much later by the road:
the trees its mirror shows are perfect, posed.

iv. ad infinitum

After she became invisible
again, it was, it seemed, inevitable
that someone had been there when she'd arrived,
that he had almost left, but was surprised
at how the weather settled on the lake
as June in January, a mistake
the retina of sky would not undo
in its pellucid glare. By then she knew
that even as she'd thought she was alone,
that even as he'd thrown the seventh stone,
it only lapped the water, skinned a face
already bared to air like any place
where circles circle, widen, dissipate:
penultimate morning, too late, too late.

v. pro vita

She waits beside the lake beneath the trees,
but it is May the bird-droned descant sends
through leaves which offer, as translation
into air, a version of a story
no one knows. The shape that words could make
are not allowed her, mated as she is
for life's sake to a movement cold and mute
as water sliding over glass, effort
ebbed in undertow she won't disclose. Now
the flak of wings is singing louder to her
than his voice, not often spent, and harsh;
he ploughs the landing, landing, turns his back:
the forest speaks in Latin to the lake,
hunched in feathers she follows in his wake.

The Rooms

*Who shall measure the heat and violence of the poet's heart
when caught and tangled in a woman's body?*
—Virginia Woolf, *A Room of One's Own*

This space is numbered. My eye counts the acres
reduced to this estate, the rows of roads, these blocks
on blocks of living place. I breathe. I shut down at night
but never dream of here. The walls are thin, sound travels
through them easier than air. The television burbles like a drunk
in my sitting room, while the radiators complain and heat goes
into corners I can't get to. Today

is the first day of spring, St. Brigid's day, the patron saint
of poets, amongst other things. I would like to think
I'd never have to vacuum again, never drag that lumpen body
over floor-rugs by its tail until, smooth as a rule
never broken, all life sucked out of them,
they give in, lie in wait for skin and hair
to pare off someone else.

The stereo kicks in. Bass notes make the bricks wilt.
I ask myself, what else is there? There's the kitchen. I hear
poison is prepared there, that clothes endure the iron after
they've been pummelled, sluiced, then, guts removed, displayed
on the gibbet in a good stiff breeze
until they have atoned for any stains.
It's also where cats spin

their marble stares on mine, say, *We are here and you are here
to mind us.* They expect me to find their food. I would
if I could find myself. It is dark in the attic.

Of course, there are bedrooms: two to sleep in, one a box
I've been known to crawl into on occasion, barely
big enough for me to swing a word in,
stretch a pen.

Despite my best efforts, the rooms swell with creatures. I blink,
they are tall. I keep blinking. I shrink. They are fabulous
jewels worth stealing. They don't bother to whisper as they plot
their own lives, their beautiful futures. Stopped dead
on the landing, at the head of the stairs,
the bathroom accosts me, it shames me
into rubber gloves: I'm afraid

I'll leave my fingerprints somewhere.

Star and Crescent Moon

The house settles.
Outside my bedroom door, a voice
not heard, usually.
I listen, feel my way
towards the landing light,

square up to the stair steps
carpet-softly, careful
of the fourth from last
one's inability
to rhyme.

In the hall, two floor rugs
float like islands,
soaking in my foot-falls
on the wooden floor.
It's quiet

as I click the kitchen door:
the cats wake up
the sleeping older dog,
the fridge purrs, water hisses
in the pipes.

In the window, full of garden
shadows, trees that whisper
assonance, a high sky has transcribed
a star and crescent moon.
I start to write.

Christina's World

after the painting by Andrew Wyeth

The land tilts away,
stretching, the yellow field yields
to the sky, the house.

Thirsty stubble grass
scratches the surface, painting
a view of the world.

Wheel tracks, half-hidden,
curve in the earth, biting off
a desolate smile.

On the horizon,
grey stone barn without a roof,
crippled on the hill.

Cold in this weather,
no smoke, without any fire,
two chimneys erect.

Shuttered windows break
the sunlight's hard exposure,
a face turns away.

The house closes off
the door's black yawning shadow,
a mouth opening.

Attic windows bulge
among the roof tiles, glass eyes
seeing everything.

Beyond the fence, land
falters, crawling to the edge,
a few short dragged yards.

After the Achter Huis

for Noeleen and Bert Van Es

i

We come out into light,
drink coffee, eat apple cake;
rain paints an acre of windows,
dissolves in the canal.
We watch a black cat leap the gap
between a houseboat and the street
where bicycles are chained in gangs
to railings, lamp-posts, anything
that can't be taken. At the bridge
a crosswind tears the map
out of my hand;
I feel as if I've lost

a layer of skin,
a present tense.

ii

Writing it down makes sense.
In the Hotel Amsterdam,
behind wine velvet curtains,
my portion of the neon sign
reads *TEL*—

On MTV a heartbeat leads
a bass guitar's wombed echoes
to a dull drum, a piano pulses notes
like blood through veins, a baby's voice
cries *Teardrop*.

iii

Earlier today, in a shop
beside the Bob Marley Café
I walk away, my bag full of bangles
and a scarf, claret-coloured
satin on one side, the other
velvet, black:

the man who sold them to me smiles,
says *Slán,*
I say *Slán Leat.*

iv

What will I take back?
The constant rain?
A view from the train
on the way to Rotterdam?
(Real windmills, clustered
in the corner of a wet field.)
The light around the easel
in Rembrandt's room?
The queue outside
The Anne Frank House?

v

The blackout clouds
the window like a swarm of flies,
the day outside is aspic, miles off.
In front of me a man tries not to cry,
a woman sobs. Beside me

in this space, a hand-stretched width
of two thin beds, a table and a chair,
my fourteen-, almost fifteen-year-old
daughter's eyes are pale
before the cut-out pictures, saved,

still pasted to the wall.

vi

But afterwards, one image rises over all:
a woman who was there describes
how, on arrival at the railway siding,
after three days, three nights standing
in the box car, they fell down
to what she knew for certain had to be
another planet,

strange, uncomfortable, lit
by the high arc searchlights
of three new moons.

Through the skin of your letter, Ann

I slide the knife.
A saucepan boils
over, clouding the window,
a canvas my daughter will draw on.
                    I still have the pictures
you sent me of your dog, moon-walking
the snow in Connecticut, neatly
sitting by the television in your apartment;
or the one you didn't send
but I see anyway—
of you and him on Sunday-morning
runs through Central Park to Dog Hill.
We never really got away
from hills, did we?
                    You ask me why
I imagine you leading a glamorous life:
it's all work you insist,
all about keeping your wits about you
on the streets of Manhattan,
and I wonder at this, later,
in my car, the windscreen emptied,
filled again as early February battens down.
                    I'm turning off
towards the Dublin Road. Ahead,
the many red-eyed demons flicker, start:
ticking over, I remain
in line. The rain stops.
The sky is sudden
deepest blue
with, all around me,
a radiance.

Roadkill

for Donal

It's dark, as dark as it gets, dark
as the night's cold heart, just after five
on a morning at the end of October.
In the dip below the hill the fields are blunt
wet velvet stretched upon the windscreen.
When you say *Look*, it's a command

barked sharp enough for me to steady, aim
my tired eyes into the perfect circle thrown there
by the headlight on my side. A flicker of fox-brush
follows another fox across a seam of open field
as if projected. The first one vanishes
into a cool obscurity

that the other, thinking on its feet, ignores
to show a noble, flip-side of a coin's half-face, deciding
he can cross us on our way to the airport.
You only tipped the brakes, you tell me
afterwards, after we hear and feel the bump
and go on in silence.

                    But what if that was me
behind the wheel, with the fox still running
past your side to mine? In an instant, black
shoe jamming as the metals trip and lock and we go
spinning towards the ditch,
while the fox switches path
and leaves us behind.

Your Hands

What is the problem here?
Is it the light of early spring, of early autumn,
or the grey air and the blue sky
compressed
into the last flat gasp
of day?

What are we talking about here?
Is it the trees, bent down, heads hard
against the breeze, or the rush
into green, into evening,
your hands on the wheel,
the miles?

What are we frightened of here?
Is it the sky, like a bowl
overturned on the earth,
the stars spilt, the stars
hard and unyielding,
the cold night?

Cat Fight

i

All yesterday it rained:
    we heard its slow fall
        breaking on the balcony

amongst the succulents'
    misshapen, wilful,
        bitter green.

The floors are slippery:
    even in the dark they glow
        the way a lake glows

underneath a low moon
    clothed in cloud,
        ringed by tall trees

miles from a road.
    The chandeliers spit
        crystal onto silver, gold,

hard surfaces, our faces:
    the mirrors throw us back
        upon each other.

ii

Across the street a sandpit in the playground browns
beneath a sheet of lights. Two lovers meet there, circle, stare—

fused, tangled, wild as cats; they leave no mark.

iii

It's late, the car park subterranean.
I walk ahead. A new day lightens
up the concrete stairwell, stretches
into Valmojada, scratches
white behind the charcoal grey of roof-slates,
trees, the highest windows.

The rain has left with nothing
left behind. The streets are sketched,
still wet, unscented
territory.

iv

In the Prado's air-conditioned, airless rooms, no sun
breaks in on walls of daughters, the *Infantas*
with their wide skirts, rainbow-daubed. We are stopped
by Goya's painting of two cats, one mottled
grey, one black:

ears flat, heads lowered, open mouths
a trap, they eye each other, hiss and cry,
stand back.

I think of water

for Mary and James English

I think of water as a word
shaped by a child, its colour
quiet flowers that surround me
draped on fences; overheard
in someone else's garden,
it is fluid-featured,
speaking in a language
I don't understand.

I think of water as a bird
above the roofs, a song-spill
into dust, a tongue of air
where dusk breathes
and the day becomes pared
down to this: a star, a moon,
an artery of concrete lane, warm
as blood between the houses.

I think of water as the world
cools on a dog's one note; at my feet
a polka-dotted cat absorbs
the kindling *crick* and *whirr*
of crickets, a flick of night-
moths pass: silently intent,
they tease the single streetlight
like a thirst.

Words to Form My Mother

i

While you were living, I could never breathe
life into you to put you on a page;
although, God knows, I tried enough to leave
your imprint there, my pen became a cage
that held you in and only let you go
like a skim of stones on water, grey
as air, in air a trace above the flow.
I could never face you in that way
you faced into each morning, eyes tight
around the light that flittered everything
you'd ever reached for as your birthright
in this world. You eluded me, to sing
and teach, to write yourself. Word by word
you slipped away from me. I never heard.

ii

I am trying (again) to write of you,
your complexities, your kind simplicity.
As usual, no word of it is true

and all the images I watered, grew,
I've cut away and do not want to see
again, as I am trying to write of you.

Your breeding blooded me and led me here through
tenements and farmers fled from Germany,
(I wonder if one word of it is true)

or if, perhaps, you never really knew
yourself, but always knew enough of me
that I would try (again) to write of you

from whose hands I long ago withdrew,
and now can't hold, won't hold the memories,
so, probably, no word of this is true.

To die, just once, is all you have to do,
you said, and understood how it would be:
I am trying (again) to write of you,
as usual, no word of it is true.

iii

Goodbye, I said, *I'll see you tomorrow;* the last words
I spoke to you that night, not quite closing the door, leaving a gap
as small as your voice had become, as small as a child.
I looked back. Head lowered, eyes already somewhere else,
in the chair beside your bed you tried to rest, your radio silent
for once. Your curtains were half-drawn against the light
that snagged in the branches of the tree outside your window;
the sky glazed over, grey subsumed into the black.

The sky glazed over, grey subsumed into the black
that snagged in the branches of the tree outside your window;
for once, your curtains were half-drawn against the light.
In the chair beside your bed you tried to rest, your radio silent.
I looked back, head lowered, eyes already somewhere else.
As small as your voice had become, as small as a child
I spoke to you that night, not quite closing the door, leaving a gap,
Goodbye, I said, *I'll see you tomorrow;* the last words.

Graffiti at Newgrange

I did not expect the ease of it
this late afternoon, the great door-stone
tied open; the entrance or exit

for those carried here before me, bone
fused with ash and whatever remained
of their jewellery, most of that stolen

by others who left only dates, names
graved among the spirals, their history
the history they soon became.

I imagine them, the light watery,
brought over the fields from the river,
the ebb and flow of it through hands, a sea

of shadow-lap and tidal shiver
weak on the walls of the passageway,
its cool dry end outside the chamber.

In the dark they turn, I turn away
towards the single breath that cleaves space,
finds a shape to fit the shortest day,

the longest night; on my expectant face
it settles. I bow my head
as if to leave, and leave no trace.

Easter

i.m. Dorothy Molloy

A rough-looking cat,
someone said,
but you didn't see it
and I didn't say it.
He didn't make a sound.
His mouth was a wound

almost closed, his eyes
bruised by a disease
you and I would have
tried to cure.
We'd have paid money.

Looking back now,
it may have been Easter,
the weather was better,
a thinner breeze
through new leaves
on the trees,

and it was evening,
darkness coming in
as we went out of the building.
You said you'd take him
home

but you had plans
for the summer, the same
was true for me;
as I walked straight ahead
towards the car park
you turned left

into Gethsemane.

Handed On

I consider the things I'll leave
after me: a ring, on my finger, last worn
by my godmother aunt
in her room at the Mater, its ruby eye alert
between two diamonds, out of its box
for the glittering occasion
that dying must be.

Or the crown-stamped wedding band
that belonged to my mother-in-law's
mother-in law. I'm told she was tall
and bold and auburn-haired;
I have my own picture. I'm certain
she never saw me
wearing it.

There's my Claddagh, heart faced
to the right place, indicating that I'm all his—
that and the blue and white stones, chosen
by everyone that year
and the Celtic circle, real silver,
my daughter paid good money for
in Kilkee.

Between all of these there's my pen:
my lucky black Amsterdam Hilton
very ordinary ballpoint.
I fool myself that it helps,
that by gently bearing down

on the page, I might leave something
there, as both of us age

and the ink runs out.

You've been this way before

You've been this way before. The road curves. The moon swerves,
staring in your windscreen open-mouthed. You

check your mirror, see the city's lights transposed. In the air
a plane tamps wary circles, kites in

as another turns its nose up, skimming streaks of light, piercing clouds.
You focus on the white line,

broken where the road slopes up in shallow turns; the sky falls
nearer as you slip the steering wheel between your fingers,

pass the metal skeleton of half-built barn. Half way up the hill
fields ripple, trees lean over, dark blue

water laps the sleeping Viking hump of Lambay. At the top, lights stop.
Nascent stars pull out. Moving back to fourth you roll

the skin of window down; the night falls in, blares past you
at Balcunnin. In another driver's pumped-up wake

notes float like ghosts. You press the radio for voices. A car comes
at you, beaming headlights. Dimmed

in Shady Lane, obscured by branches heavy-armed with leaves,
the sky has gone. You will yourself to stay

awake to pass the twin abandoned cottages that become a river
when the stream that feeds the mill's lake floods, tell yourself

you're almost there before you reach the quarry's gates: dust-
white hedges eerily familiar

as you take the final bend in one drawn breath, an echo
in the tunnel, then the roundabout, the slowing, going home.

Printed in the United Kingdom
by Lightning Source UK Ltd.
123554UK00002B/190-294/A

9 781904 556855